Embra

Humanness

Embracing my Humanness

The book information is catalogued as follows;
Author Name(s): Eloise Allen
Title: Embracing my Humanness
Description; First Edition

Book Design by Lynda Mangoro

ISBN (paperback) 978-1-914447-36-5
ISBN (ebook) 978-1-914447-37-2

Prepared by That Guy's House Ltd.
www.ThatGuysHouse.com

Embracing my
Humanness

a healing journey

ELOISE ALLEN

Foreword

I can say for definite that none of us have shared the exact same life experiences.

None of us can fully understand what another has gone through, is going through or will go through in their lifetime. But what I can say, from my own experience in relating to others in shared vulnerability, is that despite the different external experiences, many of our internal experiences share similarities- we all have emotions; we have all felt sadness, joy, pain, shame, grief, anger, disgust, and presumably many many more emotions. This we can share.

In all honesty, I feel exposed and vulnerable sharing my words but I hope that you can find some solace in this poetry, some resonation or perhaps even some understanding of a life lived by another and what it means to recognise that- that we are all living in our own realities, shaped by our upbringing and the world around us. The power of perception is truly an artistry.

This, my personal story of body, emotional, mental and spiritual healing, I share with you.

The wound is the place where the light enters you

-Rumi

Contents

root

A twinkle in your eye

Little Bear,
Do you know how much I love you?

No
Daddy Bear

I longed for most
What they couldn't give me.
Not for knowing,
For how
Can they show me love
When they don't know
How to love themselves
Because
Neither Mummy Bear
Nor
Daddy Bear
of their own
knew either.

Youth

Play with me, she squeals
between breathless cries.

Why won't you play?

Catch in the park
and swinging 'til we were sick.
A stop at the tuck shop,
Soggy ice cream fingers flick through magazines
of strange women all dolled up.
Anxious feet carry us home to play schools,
We teach our teddy bear class all things intellectual
Pausing to smear mother's lippy around sticky mouths.

A tea party to honour Friday noons,
sipping water from diddly cups
Pinkies up.
'Sit up straight, Dolly!' like good girls do.
Stolen scissors to snip barbie's hair,
Drop her from the upstairs window
to see how fast she'd fall.

Potions crafted from perfumes
Toil and trouble,
Sickly smells.
Bedtime stories of faraway lands
Yesterday can't come soon enough--
Daddy's home!
Sleep eludes us,
Walkie talkies by our bedsides
Because things go bump in the night.
Rituals to reassure;
We scream when the door's shut
It must be left ajar.

With daylight comes chaos:
Arguing adults below the stairs,
raised voices and growing pains.
School brings fruition,
an idle calm between the storms.
But skipping ropes begin to whip our ankles;
packed lunches in the bin.
Boys laugh at belly buttons
It's just boisterous banter.
Kiss-chase leaves our skin prickly,
We giggle in the bathrooms.

Then it's three o'clock,
parents at the gates watch us run out grinning.
No-one waits for me
I don't ask them to.
We walk the long way home.
Book bag down
No time for snacks,
we wander next door to play.
Neighbours' houses for nesting...

Years keep going by as motion pictures.

we
fade out.

To build her home

Home?
Somewhere to grow
somewhere to love
somewhere to cry
somewhere to share
somewhere to dream

Home is a warzone
safety is not guaranteed.

There's unrest
roaming the hallways,
Shame
leaking from the ceilings.

Discord in the dining room,
outrage in the office,
burdens in the bedrooms.

Feelings compartmentalised
Crammed into freezers
In plastic Tupperware trays.

Memories
prod and pull,
messages unearthed,
discovered from long ago.
A new home?

She'd want a home with sturdy foundations
upon which to build a life,
Brick by brick.

She'd want a bedroom for rest,
Nary a cave of isolation.

She'd want a kitchen in which to share
So much more than meals.
Where love and acceptance
is passed from plate to plate.

She'd want a staircase where the ghosts of the past
They do not sit and wait for her,
where instead,
she can climb to new heights.

She'd want a bathroom where the mirrors
no longer taunt and tease her,
where their whispers turn
from hateful hisses
to soothing sentences.

She'd want to live without limitations
to learn without judgement
to laugh without pretence
to love without fear
and to lose
And stand tall again.

She'd want to feel her heart
beat again in rhythm with her home.

For she is her home

Her body is her home.

Reparenting

Why do you weep so, little one?
Why do you shed such sorrowful tears?

Who hurt you, little one?
Who bent you until you broke?

How could they do this, little one?
How could they let you disappear?

What do you need, little one?
What do your mind and body crave?

When did it start aching so, little one?
When did you learn to face the world alone?

Where does the pain live, little one?
Where can I find the source?

Your heart, little one?
Why does it bleed this shame so?

Your gut, little one?
Why does it contort in agony?

I'm ready to hear your stories, little one.

I'm ready to hold you close.

I'm here, little one.

I am sorry.

Will-o'-the-wisp

Do not be deceived by the false promises they make,
do not embrace their deceit
as if it was lovingly packaged
for your hands to unwrap.

Beware of the string that binds the bountiful,
beware of the ground
paving the chasms of discourse.

Step back my dear
And do not go gently into that sweet night
for it is blackened by that which is not beautiful.

Friend or foe

Drifting between lullabies
no crib for a bed.
Sleep brings silence
Cocooned in a protective slumber.
If my eyes are shut
No one's there.

Dreams are hollow
Blink and they're gone.
Imprinted in the body
tucked away away
Blank spaces remaining.

Blankness
a peculiar paradigm,
Rigid and free flowing
Alive and lifeless,
Black and white.

Fit it into small square boxes
Pile them up high.
Towers of nothingness
and unobstructed pathways.

checkmate

Grandiose afflictions

The stars seem dull and lifeless now
the Burning
the Death,
their glory turned to deception.

They were dying

Hope was dying.
I wanted to be a star,
To die in a beautiful way,
Admired by others.

Everything was not the same as it had been

Life glistered before me,
solely a moment
Lost in time.
A speck
in the grand existence of humanity.

I felt empty
I felt nothing.
The strange feeling
of absolutely nothing.

I felt lost
that I was fumbling through life
Existing
but not living.

I want to be a star.

Chromatography

Time is a cruel mistress
blink

and you miss the moments

The past merges into the present
As ink running down wet paper

But ink dries.

If it's hysterical, it's probably historical

I walk through a void
once glowing with adventure
and I see anger.
A familiar friend
But I'm much more acquainted with rage.
We meet
In the hollow scope of the jaw,
Awkward and confused.
They poke me with their pincers,
a rectangular obtrusion
Dull and plastic.
Lacking in substance
Drawing from blankness
They surface and we meet.
I used to embody imagination,
Soothed by the stories unfolding.
Lusting
after heroines and happy ever afters.
And now
standing between anger and rage
I sink into their sorrow.
But
Only briefly
For anger and rage want to talk.
They tell me they don't understand why imagination had to go
I tell them,
I didn't want to grow up
So I stopped feeding my imagination.

An adventure

It teases me,
it looks me in the eyes
and chortles.

Its friends
spontaneity and playfulness
They snigger too.

It felt like trying to grasp at thin air
Trying to contain it.
Hopeless
Futile,
A cruel game I didn't wish to play.

But
I'd like an adventure.
To feel the excitement
of undiscovered lands
coursing through my veins.

To breathe in the new beginning.
A breath to ignite the fire within my belly,
a breath to shed light upon the darkness.
A breath to feel
Truly a l i v e.

To walk on untouched terrain,
Daring
to put one foot in front of the other.

To hear the foreign melodies
To speak unspoken languages,
To let go
Of the known,
of the familiar.

Embracing
Wholeheartedly
What is.

I'd like an adventure,
To transcend this well-acquainted land
To dare to be brave,
To dare to do different,
To dare to be.

The Psych ward

What they didn't tell me
Is that the screams would ring loud
Through my amoretto ears
Come day and night.

That little girls like me
They too hid their dinners
In their cardigan pockets.

That other babes still,
barely preteen,
would break bathroom mirrors
To paint their arms red.

That young boys
Could not eat
Nor walk
Nor talk
Just because.

That if we didn't finish supper
Our tomorrows
Would be rammed down our noses
And throats
In a silicone tube.

That the children I sat in school with
They were dying
All around me
Bright colours and shapes
Fading out.

That nurses watched us
Wherever we went
To catch us out
Even as we defecated.
Our lowliness laid bare.

That I would be bound
By wheels
For weeks

For my heart was far too weak.

That us youngsters
We were all hurting
From chasmic wounds
All before our 16th birthday.

That I'd be prodded
And poked,
Restrained by burly bodies
And sedated

.

That my angel friends
From that place
I would be bonded to
For years to come.

And that other voyagers
Whose paths converged,
if only for a while,
Had since abandoned ship.

Some say there are beacons out there
That lead our ships to shore
But this dunnage
Can drag us down
Unto the bitter end.

An affair with an eating disorder

She told me
she would be my friend,
that she would make me
Whole.

She whispered sweet lullaby lies to me at night
to send me to sleep.
Come day
she'd ward off anyone
who could hurt me.
I thought she was protecting me.

Slowly
she wormed her way
into my every waking minute,
now a silent scream in my ears.

She kept snatching back my hands
whenever I strayed.
She helped me
Deceive, lie, manipulate.
We were winning together at one point, so close to the end goal.

Little did I know
how close that end goal was
to death.
We were walking on a tightrope
over a deadly ravine,
And we were living off the thrill.

Then they separated us.
Tried to turn us against each other
They threatened her
Told me she wasn't my friend.
But she was all I had left in the world.

She never left my side
through it all
But she's been watching,
from the side lines.
She's been holding my hand

through the hard times.

She doesn't like change
Now she wants our relationship to be a secret,
She hides from the people I love
because they tried to hurt her.
Hurt 'us', she says.
But now she's hurting me.

She holds my head above the toilet
Pushes my hands down my throat,
She is choking me.

She shelters me from those I love
She pushes in between the cracks
filling them with hatred
guilt
and shame.

She likes to let me think
I'm in control
before she grabs the reins
and sends us charging off
into the distance,
All alone.

It's scary out here
She won't listen.

Some days I am under the illusion that she's left me
I feel a sweet
but fleeting freedom,
the pain of abandonment.
It's lonely without her.

When she returns
We argue, disagree
A continuous push and pull.

She is strong
but
I like to imagine
That I am stronger.

We lock horns more often now
Her scrawny horns leave scratches on my soul,
I like to think
I have the reins more now,
That she's the reckless bull
and I am taming her.

It's a draining relationship
and every day
is an internal struggle.

She wins some battles
Whilst I win others-
We fight to the death.

Most days she takes pride
in pinching our pockets of fat,
Scrutinising our body
and blaming me.

She has no shame,
I bathe in an ocean of shame
An ocean so deep and endless
it's overwhelming.

She tries to be my life raft in the ocean,
She comes to me on her boat
of false promises
and foolishly, I accept.
I seldom resent her
but I do pity her
for she has no one without me.

I worry about her, and where she will go.

Shadow selves

There are shadows
cast across our bedrooms
which keep us up at night.

We conjure up monsters
to scare ourselves in the dark.
The shadows who live within us
are much more terrifying,
We just don't know them yet.

These shadows have tales of woe,
Of sorrow
They protect us,
Cradle us.

Misunderstood
Labelled
Shamed
They hold our deepest fears
Shielding us from pain.

These shadows we name
to distract ourselves
from their destruction.
We try to tread a clearer path
A murky illusion,
Redirecting our fears
to external elements.

Yet
though our monsters seem frightening,
they are merely monstrous at all.

Once we begin to welcome them
Listen to them
Trust in their experience,
Their shaming label is peeled away
As a bandage from a wound.

No longer do they scare us
No longer do we ostracise them
As now
we are whole.

A Family Christmas Dinner

Families crammed around the table
The steam rises
It fills the air with a nostalgic aroma.
Knives at the ready,
Hungry souls.

Greed drains our disdain;
Substantial enough?

The pressure cooker vibrates
'We're ready!'
BANG, BANG, BANG-
Crackers echo in unison.
Crumpled paper hats to play royalty;
The 'wise' kings of the dinner table...

Voices flicker in and out
as dimming candles.
Red smeared across the table
Fingers stamped on glasses,
Meals claimed.

Grimacing smiles beneath soggy serviettes,
bellies full of pretence.

They fill silences with childish cracker jokes
Adult children doting on appearances.
As if on cue,
they laugh.

Pudding signals the finale:
Flames ablaze,
hot and sticky.
Sickly sweet,
washed down with relief.

rise

New beginnings

Petals protected beneath a deceptive shell
A dull casing wound tightly
Shielding its delicacy,
its vulnerability.

The flower inside longs to be seen,
yet
it can only be revealed in time.

Time in which to be nurtured
Time in which to be nourished.

Its fragile existence is governed by time

The petals grow restless
They begin to burst at the seams,
attempting to penetrate the walls,
both their sanctuary and their prison.

The bud shifts
loosening its grip,
letting go of limitation,
giving way to liberation.

The flower blooms:
the petals unfurl themselves,
savouring the freedom,
the light.

They can taste the sweet dew on their petals,
they dance to the rhythm of the softening breeze.

                    The flower need not resent the bud,
                            for in holding it back
                                in protecting it,
                    the bud had given rise to a new beginning:
                    A new-found sense of what it means to be free.

It's not mine

Coiled, enmeshed, entangled
It lies in my bones and breath.
Camouflaged by my skin,
seeping through my pores.
It rests between my shoulder blades
Colliding with every one of my energies.
But it's not mine.

It's leached onto my soul,
diffusing itself into my bloodstream
Snaking its way in.
But it's not mine.

My membrane was so permeable
Like a sponge I took it in
Squeezed to saturation.
But it's not mine.

Now it's floating,
suspended in time,
through my torso
Tugging and straining,
Resisting.
But it's not mine.

With trust as my shovel
I dig beneath its roots,
dragging up residual earth
and inharmonious memories.

It objects.
Clawing from the inside out.
'But where do I go?' it asks.

'I am no longer using my shovel for burying.' I reply.

It wails
Confused and uncomprehending.

I am gentle and I am firm.
I dig with patience
Weeding the shame out inch by inch
Making space for *what is mine*.

Nautical dynasties

Whispering fog
and distant dreams,
untamed desires
they spill at the seams.

Like a siren they tease
lonely sailors' woe,
Clasping, clawing-
They won't let go.

Blind ships
They wreck with ease.
Seducing currents,
That salty sea breeze.

Disoriented helms
for love-sick seamen,
A taste of reprieve,
A dormant demon.

Peace be with you

Happy tales of sorrow
Blissful tales of woe
They overlap and intertwine
until we
let
them
go

Pick your poison

It serves you
To believe
That you are to blame.

Though indeed
Blood
Is thicker than water.

How can I beseech you
Lest we not forget
Those warning signs.

I cannot save you.
We learnt this long ago
That
I can only save myself.

Limits

It took me time to believe
To accept and understand
That I too could say no.

No to this, and no to that
Without an explanation.
For I do not have to elucidate
on my reasons why.

It is my right
My human earned due.

No, indeed.

These games we play

cringe and curdle
grimace and grunt
watch her play the game

tricks and teases
shame and shunts
it always ends the same

Survival of the fittest

There was a time
When it meant life or death.
When survival was the only thing
That mattered.

In that,
We lost our self.

Because when fear
Cripples our bodies
We grasp
At paper straws
Blindly receiving
Whatever comfort comes our way.

Be it painful
Be it ultimately destructive
At once it served us.

Hollow souls
Wilting away
As decaying leaves.
Veins exposed
And fragile.

We fight
A pyrrhic rage
We flee
On legs that can't keep up
We fawn
Enshrouded by heavy expectations
And freeze
In rigid starts.

That floaty feeling

I'm giddy.
Rising up above the parapets of disillusion,
Gravity can't hold me
I'm teetering on the edge.
As a balloon with hot air rises
I too am expanding.

Though
These winds may be carrying me South
and I must go West.
Set me back on course.

I'm weightless
Descending;
It's a long way down.

People are specks,
Toy trains and Lego houses.
I am but
a distant memory.

Memories packed away
in sealed vaults and locked basements,
Festering.

Sinking stomachs
Beating ear drums and loose limbs

I'm on my way down

Building the bridge

There's energy vibrating in the bones
It's seeping into the thighs
and swirling round the chest.
It moves fast,
it slips through the fingers.
It feels intangible.

The power
the energy
it sits within the body,
but the mind is afraid of it.

The heart flutters,
I can barely make out its butterfly wings
They're swept up into this whirlwind.

The stomach churns
Nausea pushes through the oesophagus
Pauses in the throat.

This energy is trapped within me
The cognition fails to harness it
Unable to make sense of
the tingling sensations
Coursing through the bloodstream.

How do I describe the indescribable?

The mind resents the body
for it cannot control it.
It cannot surmise the energy within.

Returning to the body
is far more foreign
than I knew.
I was nescient to its instinctual rhythm
Trying instead
to compartmentalise it
into thoughts and beliefs.

The body
has been awaiting my return
to tell its story.
That instinct
That pull
was the body
asking me to return
so I could listen.

Permission to slow down
Permission to land

Hello again, *my* body.

Carnage and love await us

I hear them
Knocking at the door.
Rattling the chains
Thunderous thudding
and growing pains.

I feel them
Clawing from the inside out
Impatient and angst-ridden,
Silenced and forbidden.

I taste them
Sharp as cold metal
roused in rusty places
Bitter and jagged,
hiding in foreign spaces.

I smell them
Thick and desperate odours
cloudy and regretful
Seized by wrenching shame,
some of them forgetful.

I see them
Playing out before my eyes
thriving off the thrill
Snaking their way in,
waiting for the kill.

I hear them
I feel them
I taste them
I smell them
I see them

Lovesick people in far off places
cradled in the carnage
and the familiar faces.

A universal motion

Moons condensed into systematic spheres
Stars racing through busy skies
Energies colliding,
collapsing
and conforming.
Cyclical rhythms ebb and flow;
continuity.

Bright lights and vast, open spaces
Definite seasons define the days.
Winter protects,
Spring nurtures,
Summer provides,
Fall nourishes.

We dance,
arms thrusted towards the skies
Moving as one and many,
an unspoken agreement in motion.
We move towards, not away from,
challenging and cherishing.

We shelter beneath nature's rooves
An endless canopy of green,
our bodies merge breathlessly
Insulating,
nesting.

Our spirits wane in the light of the moon
We're exposed,
our energies entangled.
We run barefoot
Connected and contained,
free from societal shackles,
chains falling at our feet.

Our breaths are full
Plentiful and easy.
Our hearts hail the heavens,
we move as one and many.

Fallible fables

We all run
To the Edge
To see what lies beyond.
Picking up the pace
When the going gets tough
Running ourselves to the ground
In pursuit
Of perfection.

Run me ragged
I'm lagging
I can't catch a beat.
These legs can't carry me
The past
Pulls me back
Swipes me by the ankles
Flesh on flesh.

The hare can't outrun the tortoise,
Try as he might.

Shimmy

This friendship thing is a dance
At times a risky rumba
Bodies awkwardly flaring
Unsure of which way to turn,
Heads sway left
Arms sway right
Out of time to the tune
Out of the box stepping
Too close
Step back
And spin
--
Double take
Rumba turned to romp
Stomping feet
Child's play chassés
Then it's back to cha cha-ing down the stairs
Hips shimmering, hearts leading,
Wildly agreeable
Bodies acclimatising to one another
Gliding into
Our bolero
Ad astra per aspera

Let friendship be our dance
This way, then that
Sometimes to no music,
Neither regularity
Oftentimes ad lib
Still
We be the choreographers

Summer apogees

Beads of sweat
like constellations
connecting up the dots.

Sand hides from the sea
between our toes;
Hiding and seeking.

Stale sandwiches
For the gulls
Vying for a morsel.

We play scavengers
in suspect rock pools
Collecting critters.

Sunburnt flesh
stings in the sea
Salty, yet somewhat satisfying.

But what of the secrets of summer
They don't tell us.
And just like that
We grow up.

Stained bikini bottoms
Shamed faces,
Red and raw.

Burying bellies
And bodies
From naked eyes.

Hot summer nights
Tripping
Over pebbled beaches.

Drinking like those fishes
We watched beneath our feet
Dancing on the ocean floor.

Anaesthetising
In the sultry sunshine,
Rampant bodies.

And just like that
Autumn knocks
Sleepily at the door.

In a heartbeat
We are not prepared
For what had come before.

Putrid purification

The rain doesn't reach the darkest crevices of my body
The ones which yearn to be caressed
Bathed in renewal,
Cleansed and purified.

It mocks us with its moisture
The soiled parts of me
Dry and derelict,
Deserted in this hour.

Feed us, they call out
in maiming hollers.
But I do not know the stories
I am shifting through sand
Sifting through memories buried long ago.

I am nothing but.
I have forsaken my own being
And perhaps,
I am hurting.

Sandcastles

My self-worth crumbled
The words
Battered
My bricks.

They took their hammers
Unbeknownst
To the tools of their trade
And they began
To dismantle
My foundations.

I watched the pieces
fall away

Exposed
And empty handed.

No tools of my own
To build it back up.

The cement did not hold,
I am no quarry.

I envy the brick masons
In their fortresses

I yearn for that shelter.

I have but sand
For building
Intricate castles
washed away by the tide.

Daybreak

Two strangers staring up at the same sky
The cold air scratches my cheeks
Perhaps the warm air tickles yours.

It is dusk here,
The mist sweeps over the moon and gathers in pockets in the sky.
Perhaps it is dawn there,
The sun rises from its slumber and light illuminates the heavens.

We are both immersed in the transience of time.
Yet, the days and nights roll into one
Morning and noon a fading memory.

Doing something different

My heart quickens,
edging forward.
My breath wobbles.

The adrenaline sweeps the ground beneath my feet,
my whole body pulsating.

My mind is steadier,
but my body does not follow suit.
It flails in fear.

'We're doing things differently now.' I whisper.

Inner warrior

Shoulder to shoulder we stand
Bound by a bountiful belonging
far deeper than ourselves.

With unconditional love she accepts all that I am
and wills me to embrace the challenges.
To tentatively step
into the fears holding us back.

She seeks not to push me beyond limits
but to guide me
to the ever too familiar, definable edge
And while there,
we marvel at the exciting spectacle of the unknown.

She takes my hand in hers,
radiating the resilience to remobilise and re-establish.
In unspoken words she encourages,
and in her felt presence
She shields us in a swathe of awareness.

Her armour acts as a window into an ever-evolving reality
Where hope can manifest,
and where we can be emboldened
with the newfound discovery
Of choice.

Equal Rights Amendment: Women's Equality Day reflections

What inspires me
or rather,
who?

I'm perusing the metaphorical files of my mind
to pinpoint a woman who has done just that.
There have been many women whom I have met,
read about,
or listened to talk
that have given me inspiration
and whom I have thought about in awe.
But who came to my mind while reflecting?
Mulan
My childhood cherished Disney star.

But hey, there is truth in that-
To me
she represents the warrior spirit harnessed by women,
Their resilience.

Fall down seven times, get back up eight
Perseverance despite the odds.
She represents sacrificial strength
and being part of.
Part of an ancestral past that shapes us
but that which is adaptable and ever-growing.

She represents diving headfirst into the unknown
Willingly, and courageously.

She represents versatility in women
and the beauty of difference-
not only swimming against the tide
but indeed, making new waves:
These strong and powerful waves
United against the shoreline.

She represents the power of choice.
Choosing to embrace adversity
And make a change.

Women inspire
They lift up our hearts and hold them in perspective.
They are one body and spirit
formed from one another.

Grief takes guts

To love is to have lost.
I finally understand the meaning.

In grief there is loss,
heartache and pain
Some say 'joy-pain' is love.

In grief there is melancholy bliss,
a superlunary state
of fulfilment
and emptiness.
Osho says, sadness gives depth.

I have allowed grief into my heart,
into my body and soul.
I have been vulnerable
and with it
comes pain.

Brené says, if we are brave enough, often enough, we will fall.
I am falling
and I am okay with falling.
My body knows
It leads the way,
and I'm starting to trust it.

Traits of Trapeze Queens

Winding, curling, bending
round and round we go.
Momentum surges,
we rise and we fall.

Down, down, down we go
Faith in our fingers,
trust in our toes,
we rise and we fall.

Our legs sway in unison,
supporting, swinging, lifting.
Our bodies move to the rhythm of gravity,
we rise and we fall.

Pivotal moments pass us by,
we leap and we reach
With hopeful, outstretched arms,
we rise and we fall.

Up, up, up we go,
driven by the inferno churning in our chests,
propelled by possibility,
we rise and we fall.

Higher, further, longer,
the butterflies in our bellies flap and flail,
desire urges us forth,
we rise and we fall.

The trapeze's trajectory derides us
And yet, we create our own rhythmic steadiness,
mastering the mystery of movement.
Still, we rise and we fall.

The Matinee

She moulded me and sculpted me
like a plasticine figurine.
I was malleable,
I bent my spine to fit in her book.

But I was not the protagonist--
Merely an extra to her starring lead.

I spent years questioning my role,
mulling over my lines.
The words left impressions on my body.

Sometimes even now when I sleep
I recall the cues.

Interval--
Take five everyone.
But remember:
Game faces
Get in the zone.

The curtain rises
Like crashing, crimson waves
She's still on stage performing to an audience with no faces

But I have already slipped away--

I don't wait for the bows.

Skies on skies

Years float by as clouds drift in the skies
Morphing,
Shapes and colours forever shifting
Conforming, collating.

I walk beneath sand dune skies
Defined crests and grey hues,
The moon aglow.

I walk beneath cavorting creatures
Suspended in time momentarily,
We will meet again anon.
They tell tales,
Forms and figurines
Just passing through.

I walk beneath crystalline sheets
All encompassing
Emerging between breaths,
Awe-inspiring.

I walk beneath mottled skies
Prickly in pursuit
A little bumpy,
a little peculiar.

I walk beneath dull drapes
Energy spilling into gutters,
Splish
Splash
Splosh.

I walk amongst celestial bodies
Moon-bathed tracks and starlit lanes.
My head upturned,
my heart open
Half-smiling
Absorbing,
Assimilating.

Water's edge

Stubborn melodies
On shoreline sands
The surf kisses child's feet
And tender hands.

Fragmented shells
Coral and cloth
Ripening surges
As flame to the moth.

Blues coalesce
into denser tales
Egrets upon clouds
against humdrum gales.

Adieu

Is it not goodbyes that hurt us the most?
That sweet today
that turns into tomorrow.
But o, how the dusk turns to dawn
As winter turns to spring.
And how the lives shared we cherish fondly
Remembering
with ease,
the rich embrace of friendship.

The fertile void

The void Jung recalls
Fertile, is it Perls?

I am suspended in space
Proprioception at work
But not a meaning to make.

I am waiting
Hesitant and fearful
Unsure of what to make of nought.

Panic swells in my chest
Pitter patters of uncertainty
ramming at my throat.
Constricting,
not creative it seems.

Yet, I bask between blinks
A smile spread across my lips.
For I have faith
I have faith
In pure potential.
That I am an experimentalist
And
That time does tell.

Bejewelled

Dark days grow old and withered
Tiresome bodies tapping on the windowpanes,
no rest for the wicked.

The moon is heavy against the leaden veil,
A centrepiece to adorn the rooftops.
Reflecting that which is not ours
but that which haunts us still.

Grab hold of it
and draw it in close.
See the years-old prophecies,
Greet their omens
and do with them what you wish:

Paint them in gold,
brandish them,
wear them around your necks.
But I must warn you,
it hangs heavy on your heart.

Monochrome madness

Defined corners
Irregular strokes
too much
too little
Ignite the fire she stokes.

Shaky lines and rough sketches
again, again,
she etches and etches.

Party people

This, that and the other
Draped in fineries,
shrouded in silk.

They spin intricate webs
Their bodies out of sync.
Still, I see it woven
Joining up the dots,
its simplicity alluring.

Clustering bodies and voices
A hundred words make no sentence.
I forget what we were here for,
beckoned by the night sky and the laughing moon.

Smile and wave
Shake off the niceties,
formal offerings and empty glasses.

They fill them up again
And again.
Draining and discarding
Senseless substance to tickle our palates,
But it doesn't touch the sides.

The moon asks for me.
I answer
Held in his gaze.

I look behind me,
steamy windows as walls.

But there's nothing left for me inside.

Wabi-sabi

Break me with your spiteful sayings
Split me down the sides.
Leave me and return
A shell of who you once were
And rupture my being.

Have no fear for I will fill in my cracks in due course
and mend my sides with gold.
Like a master of kintsugi,
I can be beautiful again.

Acclimatising to Autumn

Days condensed into clearer night skies and dampened mornings,
the sun dragged down by the weight of the moon.
Celestial bodies adorn the late evening skies
Swimming in the dense dark hues.
The air is crisper
It clings to the cherub child's cheeks,
It smells radiant.
Grass strung with beads of dew,
Cobwebs glittering.
Trees shed outgrown skin
Marking the shift
Alongside crimson and apricot speckled leaves.
Leaves gather for comfort in piles
Swirling in the autumn breeze
Disturbed by wellie boots
Still soggy from the puddles.
They crackle and crunch.
Burrowing fauna make haste,
Collecting, gathering, storing.
We pick a peculiar pumpkin to furnish our doorstep,
Vibrant explosions erupt in the night sky
Above huddled crowds
Oohing and aahing.
They light sticks and make shapes with fire,
Precariously holding them
With gloved fingers.
Woolly hats and scarves disguise shivering bodies,
Our breath tarries in the air.
A primal lust to amass around fire becomes an honoured tradition.
Smoke furls up, up and away.
We smell the remnants of the fire on our skin,
Ashes to ashes,
Hazy clouds and lullabies.

Walls

Oh, but to what end will I keep up these walls?

They play with the periphery
As feet on a tightrope
Here
I am somewhat balanced,
cushioned if I fall.

Large nets to catch me
Laced with familiarity
Braided in monotony,
Fibres of fear.

My feet don't bend that way
Taut and tense.
They tread too carefully
Because little bones break easily.

If I trip, I could fall
and graze my knees
No flesh wounds
but still,
little children do cry.

Twenty twenty-one

All these numbing agents
Are crowding our streets
Heaving
Masses of people
No which way

Where is west?
Take me there
To see this day out.

Burnt embers raging in the skies
Anger
So much anger
Clouding the view

I cannot see beyond
The exhaust
Fumes of disarray

Where will the people go
When day is nigh
High
Above the parapets

Who is there then

To keep the world out

Through the looking glass

It is not blame
That drives my heart

These forces are insurmountable
Barely even visible
Behind rose tinted glasses.

By my own will
I cannot bring them
Over the bridge
Where the grass is not greener.

They must cross it
For want
Of the knowledge
That the grass

It was never green at all.

reach

Braving the waters

We tread these waters to keep ourselves afloat
Our bodies straining
Our mind as master
The water dense
and heavy.

We're consumed by the expanse
Daring to not look down
Resisting with decorum,
flagging inside.

No flippers for feet
No fins to float
Stiffness a superfluidity,
We pursue.

Our heads above water
between narrowing breaths.
A clockwork motion:
'Tick-tock, tick-tock,'
Hot in our heads.

Lean back into it
Let it all go
as a river mouth egressing,
Surrender to these waters.

Lonely city winters

All along the watchtower
Menacing spires as fear mongers
Blotchy ink smudged skies
promise stillness,
But no body slinks as she.

Gnarly silhouettes beckon
Long into the night
Gnawing at hungry hearts,
Insatiable appetites
always beg for more.

She sports an intrigue
A foreign feel
of long forgotten simplicities.
A wolf in sheep's clothing
Hankering for a flock.

Taking flight

The sequin speckled blue is calling out my name
Though not so transparent,
It's gossamer gilded.

Diving shapeshifters of chiffon couture,
I glide in and out
As a hummingbird.

Here
The mists are eloping
Spiralling winds rest heavy on the breeze
Melting away the impressions upon my skin,
Sheltered from the rains.

Time meanders,
Dazed and dusky headed
A cacophony of chance rallied by the fellows.

My footprints graze the shadows
Perhaps
A little less timid.

Dear Future Self,

Alone I cannot be
an impenetrable fortress against life's hardships.
I cannot be a fountain of knowledge for I do not know everything
I cannot do everything
I cannot be all things to all people.
I am one woman
one body
one mind.

I felt a funeral in my brain and wedding bells in my body
When I opened my heart to the possibility of being me
As I am,
as I stand
and as I be.
I bathed in white light
I mourned the darkness of the past
Melancholic broken pieces that didn't fit the puzzle any longer.

Because I could not stop beating myself
until I lay bare and bruised
for all the world to see.
So they could hear the lashes
I made unto my young skin.

The only ghost I ever saw
was the person I could have been
if I had been loved unconditionally.
The girl who just was
The girl who moved with magic
Without fear of what could be.

And so, I wish you
with a heart ajar,
an ever-expanding essence
And true acceptance.

All my love,

Eloise

It's not about you, it's about me

There's a rising
In my system
A pulsating niggle
That just won't
Step back

I condemn the other
For fear I am alike

I justify my reasoning
Going round
And
Round
In circles

I belittle the other
To curb the all-consuming hunger
Of my own inadequacy

I resent the other
For they can do
What I cannot

Self-searching
I find
I can too
Learn how
to show up in the world

The first step
Awareness

The second
Compassion.

Empathy

I don't believe in
The hierarchy of suffering.
It births shame
Nourishing shoulds and shouldn'ts
Neglecting what is real for us
In this moment
Regardless of any other.

I was told as a child
To be grateful
That I am lucky
Because I have more than some
But I've come to realise
That it's not about what we did have
Rather
What we didn't.

An angel once told me
That connection is as essential to our survival
As food and water.

I should not have had to
I should have had

Mirror me
Or
I'll mirror you
Between splintered shreds of glass
I will lie
To ensure my survival.

Love is

Love is

Not neglecting your own needs
In the face of another.

It is saying no
Out of respect
For you
And for me.

It is giving
without expectation,
And taking
without needless guilt.

It is sharing our truths
In vulnerability
Despite the fears.

It is letting them know
That beneath the anger
I am so very afraid.

Love is

Courage

In the age of editing

We're hoodwinked
into believing
that to be beautiful
means
to have curves
in all the right places.
To have unblemished skin
All squeaky clean.
To fit into
this
one-dimensional box
Cramming our limbs
into air-depleting spaces.
No room
for stained souls.
Rub out the pencil marks
and fill them in
with black fine liners.
Bend your back
until it snaps
like a whip unto the flank.
But ask yourself this,
When our skin is sallow
When our hair is thin
and our shape is but a squiggle,
Where
upon that blank sheet of paper
did you fill it in
with colour?

The real epidemic

Don't cry
They don't want to see your tears
Washing their stained-glass windows
Built around Their sacred spires
Of disillusionment

Don't speak
About your hardships
Held up against a tapestry of social stratum
Fine fibres pulled taut,
Your verbose unwelcome here

Batten down the hatches
Build your walls up sky high,
Don't let them see you cry
Your humanness,
Unwelcome here

Run

We drove through the gully
Listening to Snow Patrol
The wind fresh in our breath.
A stream of interconnectedness
With nature,
With ourselves.

The uplift of awe resonating
from the radio
and between our hearts.
A scenic journey
Where lost children crossed tracks
If only briefly.

We spoke not words
But hummed
In tune,
Attuned.
Our systems satisfied by love.

Though teary-eyed
We wallowed not in woe
But in the art of living for another
The parent-child bond
Syncing to the song.

Character defects

It says we're defected

I admit defeat
I admit powerlessness
But I refuse the notion
That I am in some way flawed.

I know too much
I see the fraying edges,
That those curtains
Did not block out all the sunlight
Despite their trying

Addiction
Is a cunning master,
A mistress of jiggery-pokery
But I know
She's trying to offer some relief
In a room with no windows.

Ragamuffins scorned
Lazy.
Unmotivated.
They didn't help themselves.

I ask you

Stop

Take a look
At their room,
Do you fear
What you see
In that mirror?

We are all trying our best
With what we have
To quell the agony inside.

It is not bitter hearts
That mend broken ones.

It's not glamour

I slipped and fell
Headfirst
Down on my knees
Retching

Tears rolling down my face
Pooling round my mouth
Snot and Spit and Tears

I look to the mirror
Pain swelling in my cheeks
Chunks of dignity chipped away
Like plaster on a drying wall
My body crumbles

Get it out
Rid me of this fullness
Of feeling,
I am aching

Swollen with shame
Pipes too narrow
For this holding

Get it out
So I can be again perfect,
Perfectly in pieces

Feel

The rain caressed my body
Between a thousand kisses
Planted on my cheeks.

Touched
By melancholy
Drifting on the wind.

A drowsy day
Rolling into evening
Too soon for pause.

Left alone
With
Me
Myself
And
I

A story I made up

That dewy grass
Kissed our souls,
We walked the grounds with Gandalf.
A garland of fairy lights lit up the skies,
The bunting bandaged the trees.

Our laughs echoed
Out beyond the boundaries,
We wore crowns of daisies
And got lost in the labyrinth.

Do you remember
The twenty first night of September?
Burning sage and sandalwood
To chase away the traces.

Or when Mr. Barn Owl soared above
Our clouds of cigarette smoke
Thick in the early summer air.

Better still
Drumming to the beat
of one man's tune,
They called him Stem.

Snowball fights inside
With the Dancing Queens,
By evening
Our bellies sore from laughter.

I heard once
That
Wistful winds
Murmur happy memories,

And I believe it so.

I am no reservoir

Today I was a lake
Of vast stillness,
Expansiveness
Contained.

I moved
With the element
My limbs mimicking the flow,
Staccato at first
Before the waters settled.

Fluidity swam round the edges
Cautiously teetering
On the periphery.

I painted the blues on white
Fingertips smudging the sides,
I danced with myself
Beside the lake.

Close your eyes
She said
Feel into the water
How does it move?
What does it feel like
To be
This lake

Jailhouse

They spit out words
Before our feet
Nary looking us in the eye.
I stand as a china doll
Fingernails scraping me
As chalk on a blackboard.
Toes curling in disgust,
Teeth grinding
Between pursed lips
Skin crawling,
Itchy and ravenous.

Braced

I writhe
As a creature in a weighted net,
Primal instincts overcome me
But my screams don't reach
The farthest corners
Of my porcelain body.
They do not satisfy
These animal urges.

How I want to rid myself
Of all these feelings,
Shed this skin
And watch it all bleed dry.

Messengers

Today I woke up to sadness,
She likes to disguise herself
As low
As she can.
Her senses dull,
Her instinct to hide
She seeks reprieve
In isolation.

By late morning
Agitation had arrived
She is visceral
With talons urging
To rip out our insides.
To split from our body,
Leaving our feathers to moult.

Come noon
Hope smiled in the creases of our lips
She is shy
Doe-eyed and dimpled,
Tenderly peeking out
At the big wide world.

Fear beckoned at lunch
Clothed in thought
Offering an appetiser,
She can't sit still for long
Out the door in minutes.

Dusk brought loneliness
Clinging to my chest
She's one of the youngest,
Pre-verbal.

Late evening
Settled inside,
I tucked my children in.

Each day I meet another,
A familiar face
Or a long-lost memory
Comes forth
At once
It was chaos
And at times
It still is
But I know them
Now
I know they're messengers.

Five words, six syllables
A blow to the stomach
Air knocked from my lungs
Gasping
Cradling the pains
Burrowed in a tiny ball,
Foetal throbbing
Thoughts whirring through this time machine
Jolting me back,
This is no zephyr

Five words, six syllables
Clutching tender open wounds
Bandages fallen at my feet,
Exposed here to this deluge
Of raw emotion,
Heart-wrenching agony

Five words, six syllables
I drag up buckets from my well
I am phrases
To fill me up,
Draining the soiled water.

They're not my beliefs
I give them back,
I dare not be your repository

Newsflash

Can you give yourself permission
To let yourself off that hook
So far from reach
That you're always striving
For that something, or other

For in that reaching, was there pain?

Because what if it's okay
That today you're not

What if it's okay to stay in bed today
Safe
For that is still enough

What if it's okay to ask for help
Brave
You are still enough

What if it's okay to ask yourself
What do I need today?
And what if it's okay to not know right now

What you do today or don't do is no measure
Your existence-
That is your worth

I hate to break it to you my darling
But you're not a human doing

You're a human being

Let me be

As a girl
I understood not
Of the value of my body
I let it decay
As a vessel
Harbouring no passenger
I was not shown
How to be a woman
Womanhood was folklore
Amidst a myriad of disguise
I stamped my feet in scorn
At the audacity.

I knew not
Of the magnetism of my body
The surplus electricity
A dimming bulb
My sexuality unexplored
Toned to fit another's tune.

I will not be a marble block
To take their chisel to
So they can carve their own figures
Just the way they like them,
My nipples will not stand to attention
At their command
My breasts will not mould
To their hands
My lips will not purse
For their words
Spat out at my feet

I was not made for their intrigue,
My body squirms in dismay
Sexual liberties
Made for them
Now I

I am not six of one
Half a dozen of the other
I am a whole human

The rope swing

The swing sits lopsided,
Droopy eyed and weary.
Her bark is no worse than her bite
She is sleepy
Basking in the afternoon sunshine,
Tickled by the wind.
She is no stranger to this captor
But she misses indulging
Play
Left her empty handed
Rotting in her cell

Don't let it eat away at you
He said
Not like it has her
He said.

So, the swing sits
Lulled by her dreaming
Bright eyed
No bushy tails yet
Her shadows chasing away the light
Then
Pitter patter came little feet
Eager, somewhat cautious
Sweeping through the trees
Brushing the bark anew
Clearing
The foliage from the forest floor,
Pitter patter
Pitter patter,
Faster came the little feet.

Paint by numbers

Pick a colour
Any colour
Smear your skin
War paint
Lines marking our cheeks
Identities defined
Or not
By the marks we make.
Streaks of blues and reds
Greens, pinks, oranges, yellows
Blacks and whites
Silvers and golds
Every shade, every hue.

Pick a colour
Any colour
Your palette as your landscape
Your body as your canvas
Battle grounds sodden
Drenched in colour
Saturated in secrets
Flaking from our faces

You,

An artist.

You are cancelled

Control alt delete
As simple as that
To remove a *human being*

How

   Did we get here?

The black mirrors have taken us
Hostage
Or
Did we let them?

Selling our souls to Hades
Swimming in code
Hiding
Behind screens
Calling ourselves mighty
Keyboard warriors
Tap tap tapping away
Always
Seeking more.

What's your Instagram
Not double-digit followers? Ouch.
Did they like my photo…

Do they like me?

You've become disposable.
Join the cult
March
Side by side the screens
Stamping out mistakes
With the touch of a finger
Scraping the barrels of connection
With zeros and ones

Never mind their feelings
There's no flesh to be seen
It's all too easy

Control
alt

delete.

I'll meet you there

I turned to my therapist
And I said
I know what Rumi means
I understand what he meant when he said
Out beyond ideas of wrongdoing and rightdoing there is a field…
I'll meet you there

Our truths are subjective
Interwoven in our fascia
So now you see
Through a clouded lens
Not at one with the object
As Patanjali too noted,
Our minds not yet flawless diamonds
Though the many
We deem our reality truth.
We are but uncrystallised carbon,
Metamorphosing.

Laws are born
Collective rights and wrongs
What if I choose to think different
Am I then
Wrong
Because you deem my diamond a little rougher round the edges?
Because my diamond does not cut like the others?
Perhaps
My diamond's free electrons
Don't fit
With the regular lattice

How extraordinary,
What a privilege to believe
In truth.

Interfaced

When did the world
Turn to black and white
This monochrome lens
Zooms in
From only one angle

Sharp tongued
Not quick to question
The grey area
Forming transparent beliefs
Reading the lines as just so
No between
Just straight marks made on paper
Stubs of graphite
Incising
Into one another

When did we stop listening?
Words poised
At the ready
For quick fire
Pouncing on the others' tongues
Sentences hung in mid air
Splayed across the tables
Unfinished, cast aside
For the right ones
Or so they think

Do they not know
There are seven point seven billion sides
To every story

Vacant

Bland, I called it
Putting a name to no face
Beige, Oatmeal, Limp
Mechanical limbs tugged down
The weight of the world
Heavy
On sore shoulders

Cling film I named it
Moving towards
Bouncing back confused
This transpicuous barrier elusive,
Look but can't touch

Detaching
As a puppet hanging by fraying thread,
I am sagging
Beneath a flimsy coat of fine
Okays
Goods

Mixed messages between droopy eyelids
Be strong it says,
But this kind of strong leaves me weak
That I know
And yet
I keep going

I catch myself
When I fall

I pick myself up
Pat myself down
Dust myself off

And I'm dead beat
Now I ask
Can someone help

Meditation

Swooping in and out
Tempestuous wings
Spiralling down
Bring them back
To land
Caressing those feathers fondly
Riotous or recluse
It's what brains do

Dearest A

Oh, my dear
There are better days to come
Catching rides on the sunrays
A thousand kisses from the rain
Earthy skin on skin
My hand holds yours

I have got you

The herd

Who are you
If you stripped yourself bare
Layer upon layer
Of societal labels
Politics, gender, race, class, sexuality...
Identity tags unhooked

What makes you *you* then?

Are we but a product to be dispatched
Tagged like cattle

I too branded myself
I too have been branded
Hot angry iron on flesh
Grouped like animals
Stringing bells of shame around necks
A sombre tintinnabulation,
Blame vibrating through pores
An outlet it appears
To squeeze them through the gates,
Barred in

I ask
What is this equality we are searching for
What does identity mean to each of us

Or are we all just taking ourselves to the slaughterhouse?
I deny that this pasture isn't big enough for us all.

I am
When stripped bare
Essence

I am
Life force

I am
Creation itself

Who are you?

Rebirth

And now,
we reach an ending.
Not in the traditional sense
Of the word,
But in and of itself
As just that.

For in every ending
There is a beginning.
Cyclically
It all rolls into one.

A container for growth
Be the circle of life,
Blending in the tones
Of transformation.

Not you
Nor I
Can draw
A perfect circle
By our own hands.

It is up to the Divine
The forces of nature,
Creation
And destruction
To free our souls.

Lightning Source UK Ltd.
Milton Keynes UK
UKHW011831050422
401140UK00004B/1128